SCENE BY SCENE COMPARATIVE WORKBOOK HL17

FOSTER

by Claire Keegan

Theme/Issue - Relationships

Literary Genre

General Vision and Viewpoint

Copyright © 2016 by Amy Farrell.

All rights reserved. No part of this publication may be reproduced, distributed or transmitted in any form or by any means, including photocopying, recording, or other electronic or mechanical methods, without the prior written permission of the publisher, except in the case of brief quotations embodied in critical reviews and certain other noncommercial uses permitted by copyright law. For permission requests, write to the publisher, addressed "Attention: Permissions Coordinator," at the address below.

Scene by Scene
11 Millfield, Enniskerry
Wicklow, Ireland.
www.scenebysceneguides.com

info@scenebysceneguides.com

Foster Comparative Workbook HL17 by Amy Farrell. —1st ed.
ISBN 978-1-910949-40-5

Foster Comparative Study Workbook

This workbook is designed to help Leaving Certificate English students become familiar with the Comparative Study modes and to understand how each mode may be applied to *Foster*.

The Comparative Study Modes at Higher Level for 2017 are:

Theme/Issue

The theme covered in this workbook is Relationships. This theme can be applied to any relationship in a text and covers love, marriage, friendship and family bonds.

Consider the complexities of relationships and the impact they have on characters' lives.

Literary Genre

This mode refers to the way the story is told.

Consider aspects of narration such as the manner and style of narration, characterisation, setting, tension, literary techniques, etc.

The General Vision and Viewpoint

This mode refers to the author's outlook or view of life and how this viewpoint is represented in the text.

Consider whether the text is bright or dark, optimistic or pessimistic, uplifting or bleak, etc.

How Does it Work?

This workbook has three parts, one each for Theme/Issue (our chosen theme for study is Relationships), Literary Genre and General Vision and Viewpoint. Each part has three sections: Know the Text, Know the Mode and Compare the Texts.

Know The Text

These questions are on the *Foster* text and refer specifically to this novel. Through answering these questions you will get to know the text well, while also getting a feel for the Comparative Study mode the questions relate to.

Know the Mode

These questions use 'mode' specific terms and phrases and are intended to help prepare you for tackling exam questions. They focus on the mode itself, rather than the text you have studied. You apply your knowledge of the text to the mode in question.

Compare the Texts

These questions ask you to compare your texts under specific aspects of each mode. It is important that you get used to the idea of comparing and contrasting your chosen texts, as this is what the Comparative Study is all about. It is good practice to think about your texts in terms of their similarities and differences within each mode.

This approach is designed to prevent 'drift' between modes and focuses on analysis and personal response, rather than summary.

Theme/Issue - Know the Text

1 Does the girl have a good relationship with her father?

2 Does the girl have a good relationship with her mother?

3 Does the girl have a loving family?

4 What **strengths** do you see in the girl's relationships with her family?

KNOW THE TEXT

5 What **weaknesses** or problems do you see in the girl's relationships with her family?

6 Are these positive or negative relationships? Use examples to justify your view.

FOSTER - THEME/ISSUE - RELATIONSHIPS

7 How do the Kinsellas (her aunt and uncle) treat her when she comes to stay with them?

8 Who benefits from this arrangement?

KNOW THE TEXT

9 Does she miss her parents when she goes to stay with her aunt and uncle?

10 Are her aunt and uncle good foster parents? Explain, giving examples.

11 Are they a positive or negative influence on her?

12 Do the Kinsellas love the girl?

KNOW THE TEXT

> **13** How well do the speaker and her parents **communicate**, interact and understand one another??

> **14** How well do the speaker and the Kinsellas **communicate**, interact and understand one another?

FOSTER - THEME/ISSUE - RELATIONSHIPS

15 How does learning about her cousin's death impact on the girl's relationship with the Kinsellas? Does it make sense of anything for you?

16 Do the girl's parents know her well? Give examples in your answer.

17 Do the girl's aunt and uncle know her well? Give examples in your answer.

18 Does the girl love her parents or foster parents most? Explain your view.

| 19 | Does it matter who she loves most? Is this difficult for the girl? |

| 20 | How do the girl's relationships with her parents **change** and **develop** during the novel? |

KNOW THE TEXT

21 How do the girl's relationships with her aunt and uncle **change** and **develop** during the novel?

22 Who matters most to the girl? Explain your choice. How does this make you feel?

FOSTER - THEME/ISSUE - RELATIONSHIPS

23 How do the girl's family treat her when she returns home?

24 Has she benefitted from her time with the Kinsellas?

Theme/Issue - Know the Mode

25 Are relationships in this text generally **positive** (warm, supportive, nurturing, genuine) or **negative** (cold, cruel, destructive, false)?

26 What makes relationships in this text complicated and **difficult**?

KNOW THE MODE

27 What would **improve** relationships in this text?

FOSTER - THEME/ISSUE - RELATIONSHIPS

28 How do relationships **change** during the story?

KNOW THE MODE

29 What did **you learn** about relationships from reading this novel?

30 Are relationships **portrayed realistically** in this text? Make use of examples to support the points you make.

KNOW THE MODE

31 Are relationships in this story **interesting** and **involving**?

32 Did anything about the theme of relationships in this text **shock, upset** or **unsettle** you?

33 What is the **most signficant relationship** in this text?
What makes it so significant and important?

FOSTER - THEME/ISSUE - RELATIONSHIPS

34 Do relationships in this story bring characters **happiness** or **sorrow**?

KNOW THE MODE

35 Choose **key moments** from this story that highlight relationships in the text.

Theme/Issue - Compare the Texts

36 Were relationships in *Foster* more positive and supportive than the relationships in your other texts? Give specific examples.

37 Rank the relationships you have studied in your various texts from most positive to most negative. Add a note to explain your choices.

COMPARE THE TEXTS

38 Were relationships in *Foster* the most engaging and interesting that you have studied? Explain your choice.

39 Rank the relationships you have studied in your various texts from most interesting to least interesting. Add a note to explain your choices.

40 Did you **learn most** about the theme of relationships from this text or another text on your comparative course?

FOSTER - THEME/ISSUE - RELATIONSHIPS

> **41** What **similarities** do you notice in the theme of relationships in this text and your other comparative texts?

COMPARE THE TEXTS

42
What **differences** do you notice in the theme of relationships in this text and your other comparative texts?

COMPARE THE TEXTS

Literary Genre - Know the Text

43 How is this story told? (Consider the novel format).

44 Why is the story told in this way? What is the effect of this?

KNOW THE TEXT

45 Is **the girl** a **good** choice of **narrator**? Explain your view.

46 The girl doesn't fully understand everything that is going on. How does this add to the story?

FOSTER – LITERARY GENRE

47 Is the news of her cousin's death an **unexpected twist**? What hints are there that something tragic has happened in the Kinsellas' lives?
Does this development add to the story?

48 We never learn the girl's name. Why did Claire Keegan choose to leave her nameless?
What is the effect of this?

KNOW THE TEXT

| 49 | How does the **setting** of the Irish countryside contribute to the story? |

| 50 | How does the author create the sense that the girl belongs in her new home? |

> **51** How does the author create a sense of the girl's character? Did you like this character?

> **52** How did the author create a sense of the girl's father? Did you like this character?

KNOW THE TEXT

53 How did the author create a sense of the girl's mother? Did you like this character?

54 How did the author create a sense of Kinsella, the girl's uncle? Did you like this character?

55 How did the author create a sense of Edna, the girl's aunt? Did you like this character?

56 Is this a novel about loneliness, grief, love or something else?

| 57 | How does the **chapter structure** affect the way the story is told? |

| 58 | What different aspects of the text combine in the final chapter to make it **emotional** and moving? |

59 *Foster* has been described as "beautiful, strange and moving". Do you agree with this assessment?

Literary Genre - Know the Mode

60 Did **you** enjoy the **storyline** of the text?
Was it exciting/compelling/tense/emotional?
Why/why not?

61 Is there just one **plot** or many plots?
What connections can you make between the storylines?

62 What three things interested **you** most in the story?

KNOW THE MODE

63 Are **characters** vivid, realistic and well-developed?

64 Do **you** empathise or **identify** with any character(s)?
Did you become involved in this story or care about the characters? What made you identify with or connect with characters? Use examples.

65 Who was your **favourite character**?
What aspects of this character did you enjoy?

KNOW THE MODE

66 Consider the girl as the novel's **heroine**. What made her a **memorable** or **interesting** character?

67 Who was your **least favourite character**? What aspects of this character did you dislike? What made them a memorable or interesting character?

KNOW THE MODE

68 Is the story humorous or tragic, romantic or realistic? Explain using examples.

69 To what **genre** does it belong?
What aspects of this genre did you enjoy?
Is it Romance, Thriller, Horror, Action/Adventure, Historical, Fantasy, Science-fiction, Satire, etc.?

70 How does the author create **suspense**, **high emotion** and **excitement** in the text? What **techniques** does she use to good advantage?

71 Consider the author's use of **tension** and **resolution** in the novel. What are the major **tensions/problems/conflicts** in the text? Are they **resolved** or not?

72 Did the author make use of any striking patterns of **imagery** or **symbols** to add to the story?

73 How does the author make use of the **unexpected** in this story? What did this add to the text? (Think about key moments here.)

KNOW THE MODE

74 What is the **climax** (high point) of the story?

75 What did **you** think of this moment?
How did it make **you feel**?

76 Comment on the **language** of the novel. How does **dialogue** add to the story?

77 Comment on the **setting** of the novel. Consider time, place, and specific locations such as Gorey town. How does setting add to your understanding of the characters and their story?

78 Was anything about this novel **moving** or **emotional**?

Think of moments in the novel that you responded to. What made them moving? How did this add to the story?

79 On a scale of one to ten, how much did you enjoy the **ending**? What was satisfying/unsatisfying about it? Was anything left unanswered?

80 The experiences of seeing a play, reading a novel and viewing a film are very different.
What aspects of the **novel form** worked well in this story, in your opinion?

81 What did **you** like about **the way** the story was told?
*Mention aspects of storytelling and literary techniques that **you** found enjoyable. Refer to key moments.*

82 Identify **key moments** in the novel that illustrate Literary Genre (the way the story is told). Clearly **define literary techniques/aspects of narrative** in your analysis.

KNOW THE MODE

Literary Genre - Compare the Texts

83 Did **you** like the way this story was told more than your other comparative texts?
State what you enjoyed most about each.

84 Is *Foster* more **exciting** than your other texts? *Consider tension, suspense, pacing, conflict and the unexpected.*

85 Are **characters** more engaging in this novel than in your other texts?
Refer to each of your texts in you answer.

COMPARE THE TEXTS

86 Is the **setting** more effective in telling this story than in your other texts?
Refer to each of your texts in your answer.

87 Is this story more **unpredictable** than your other texts? Refer to each of your texts in your answer.

COMPARE THE TEXTS

88 Did this novel have greater **emotional power** than your other texts?
Was this emotional power created in a more interesting way here or in a different text?

89
What **similarities** do you notice in the Literary Genre of this novel and your other comparative texts?
Mention specific aspects of narrative.

COMPARE THE TEXTS

90

What **differences** do you notice in the Literary Genre of this novel and your other comparative texts?

Mention specific aspects of narrative.

COMPARE THE TEXTS

General Vision and Viewpoint - Know the Text

91 How do you feel about the girl being sent to live with her aunt and uncle?

92 What is life like for her at home with her parents and siblings?
What is your response to this?

KNOW THE TEXT

> **93** Is life better or worse for her with the Kinsellas?
> How do you feel about this?

> **94** Is the girl loved and wanted in this story?
> Is this a positive or negative comment on life?

95 What does learning about the death of their son reveal to you about the Kinsellas' lives?

96 Why did Mildred tell the girl about this tragedy? What is your reaction to the way she broke this news?

KNOW THE TEXT

97 What is the atmosphere like as Kinsella and the girl go walking by the shore at night?
How did you feel as you read this section?

98 How do the adults in the story treat one another?

FOSTER - GENERAL VISION AND VIEWPOINT

99 Are the girl's parents happy with their lot in life? Are the Kinsellas happy and content?

100 Did you want the girl to stay with the Kinsellas? Explain your response.

KNOW THE TEXT

101 How do you feel, reading about the girl's return home?

102 Is the girl's future promising?

103 Did you anticipate a happy ending?

104 Is this a happy ending?

KNOW THE TEXT

105 How does the closing section make you feel?

106 What is Claire Keegan telling us about life in this story?
What is Claire Keegan's message?
Is her outlook positive or negative, in your view?

General Vision and Viewpoint - Know the Mode

107 Identify bright/hopeful/optimistic aspects of the novel.

108 Identify dark/hopeless/pessimistic aspects of the novel.

109
Is this text **optimistic** or **pessimistic**? Explain. *Consider characters' happiness, imagery, atmosphere, future prospects, etc.*

110
On a scale of one to ten, how optimistic is this text?

111 Identify the **aspects of life** that the author concentrates on.
Are they positive or negative?
Consider distance, secrecy, isolation, grief, love, etc.

112 What **comments** do characters make on their **society** and the problems they're facing?

KNOW THE MODE

113 Are characters happy or unhappy?

114 What makes characters in this story happy and fulfilled?

FOSTER - GENERAL VISION AND VIEWPOINT

115 What makes characters in this story unhappy and unfulfilled?

116 Are **relationships** destructive or nurturing? What do they reveal about life, as we see characters supported/thwarted in their efforts to grow/mature?

117 Are **imagery** and **language** bright or dark in the text? (Tone of the text)

118 What is the **mood** of this text?

KNOW THE MODE

119 What does this story **teach us about life**?
What do we learn about life's hardships? Are struggles overcome? Is determination rewarded? Is life difficult or joyful?

120 How do you **feel** as you read this novel?
Refer to key moments to anchor your answer.

121 How do you **feel** at the **end**?

122 Are **questions** raised by the text **resolved** by the end?
Are they resolved **happily** or **unhappily**?

123 Are **you hopeful** or **despairing** regarding the prospects for human **happiness** in this story?
Are characters likely to be happy?

FOSTER - GENERAL VISION AND VIEWPOINT

124 Identify the **key moments** in the novel that illustrate the General Vision and Viewpoint of the text.

KNOW THE MODE

General Vision and Viewpoint - Compare the Texts

125 Is life happier for characters in this story than in your other comparative texts? Explain.

126 Do characters in this text face more obstacles and difficulties than in your other texts?
Who struggles most?

127 Are characters in this text **rewarded more** for their struggles than in your other texts?
By overcoming adversity, do they achieve true happiness and contentment in a way that is not realised in your other texts?

128 Is this the brightest, most hopeful and triumphant text you have studied? Explain why its message is more or less positive than your other texts.

129 Which of your chosen texts was the bleakest and most upsetting or depressing?
Explain why it was more negative than your other texts. What made them more positive?

130

Plot your three texts on a scale of one to ten, from darkest (most pessimistic) to brightest (most optimistic). Add points to explain their position.

131 What **similarities** do you notice in the General Vision and Viewpoint of this text and your other comparative texts?

COMPARE THE TEXTS

132 What **differences** do you notice in the General Vision and Viewpoint of this text and your other comparative texts?

COMPARE THE TEXTS

www.ingramcontent.com/pod-product-compliance
Lightning Source LLC
Chambersburg PA
CBHW050714090526
44587CB00019B/3371